WORKBOOK FOR

ATLAS OF THE HEART

MAPPING MEANINGFUL CONNECTION AND THE LANGUAGE OF HUMAN EXPERIENCE

BY

BRENÉ BROWN

GREENPRINT PUBLISHERS

Copyright © 2021 by GREENPRINT PUBLISHERS

ISBN: 978-1-63809-020-5

All rights reserved. This book or any portion thereof may not be reproduced or used in any manner whatsoever without the express written permission of the publisher. For more information, requests, or recommendations you can reach us on pocketbooksdesign@gmail.com

Disclaimer:

Terms of Use: Product names, logos, brands, and other trademarks featured or referred to within this publication are the property of their respective trademark holders and are not affiliated with this publication. The information in this book is meant for educational and entertainment purposes only, and the publisher and author make no representations or warranties concerning the accuracy or completeness of these contents and disclaim all warranties such as warranties of fitness for a particular purpose. This book is an unofficial summary, and analytical review meant for educational and entertainment purposes only and has not been authorized, approved, licensed, or endorsed by the original book´s author or publisher and any of their licensees or affiliates.

Table of Contents

HOW TO USE THIS WORKBOOK 4

INTRODUCTION 5

    WHO SHOULD USE THIS WORKBOOK? 6

    WHAT'S IN IT FOR ME AND WHY IS IT IMPORTANT? 6

#1 PLACES WE GO WHEN THINGS ARE UNCERTAIN OR TOO MUCH 7

#2 PLACES WE GO WHEN WE COMPARE 12

#3 PLACES WE GO WHEN THINGS DON'T GO AS PLANNED 16

#4 PLACES WE GO WHEN IT'S BEYOND US 21

#5 PLACES WE GO WHEN THINGS AREN'T WHAT THEY SEEM 25

#6 PLACES WE GO WHEN WE ARE HURTING 30

#7 PLACES WE GO WITH OTHERS 35

#8 PLACES WE GO WHEN WE FALL SHORT 40

#10 PLACES WE GO WHEN THE HEART IS OPEN 49

#11 PLACES WE GO WHEN LIFE IS GOOD 54

#12 PLACES WE GO WHEN WE FEEL WRONGED 59

#13 PLACES WE GO TO SELF-ASSESS 64

HOW TO USE THIS WORKBOOK

This workbook was created with one overall goal – with the right language, you can define, identify, and change your life. This workbook will help you understand your emotions **and act** (not react) **rightly.**

The world we live in is full of events that will remind us of the emotions on the lower such as pain, sorrow and sadness. This makes it easier for us to shut ourselves inward and live in our heads while we are disconnected from those who love us as well as the other beautiful experiences of life.

With this workbook, you can be sure that you'll connect with others. You can understand yourself, know what you need, what you want and share it with those who deserve it.

However, this is conditional. The previous paragraph can only apply to you when you answer the questions truthfully. Some people have lived in denial for too long that it's impossible to know who you are. This is why I'll advise you to revisit the questions after one month and after every three months.

At the beginning of each section, you'll find key takeaways to refresh your mind and help you understand how you need to see yourself and the world around you.

I'm sure you'll not only love and enjoy these exercises; you'll also get the workbook for your friends.

INTRODUCTION

Atlas of the heart by Brene Brown will help you understand yourself, and spot who you are and what you need in the midst of conflicting emotions. You'll be able to take in all experiences that come your way without losing or hiding yourself in fear, shame or guilt.

You'll be able to spot and identify the emotions you feel and why you feel that way. This will help you live and not just exist (which is what many people do). You'll learn how to connect with others and show other emotions that help you make a mark in the life of others.

You'll be able to understand how and why some things happen so you can name them, think about them and make choices that reflect your values and your heart.

WHO SHOULD USE THIS WORKBOOK?

Everyone deserves a chance to use this workbook.

This workbook is meant for anyone who is tired of living in the shadows, not understanding yourself and those tired of not living up to their true values. It is also for those who live connectedly so they understand themselves better and live valuable lives.

WHAT'S IN IT FOR ME AND WHY IS IT IMPORTANT?

I urge you to read and practice what you've learned by using this workbook. When you do, you'll feel alive. You're not moved or shaken unnecessarily and you're sure of whom you are.

No one can push you into fear or guilt or make you feel ashamed of your pain. Your emotions are an expression of who you are and it deserves the right to be expressed. You'll find out how to express it properly

You'll shed off anxiety, fear, shame, guilt and other similar emotions so you become a better person.

You'll learn how to establish and maintain connection with the people in your life.

You'll be able to build grounded confidence.

You'll be able to practice embodiment and do away with disembodiment.

All these and many more are what you stand to gain and the reasons why this workbook is important.

#1 PLACES WE GO WHEN THINGS ARE UNCERTAIN OR TOO MUCH

Here are a few key takeaways from this section

We feel stressed when we evaluate environmental demand as beyond our ability to cope successfully.

When stressed, your emotions respond to how your thoughts can handle the situation.

Overwhelmed means an extreme level of stress, an emotional and/or cognitive intensity to the point of feeling unable to function.

Non-doing when overwhelmed makes sense because we don't process information properly when we are overwhelmed and this leads to poor decision making.

When you feel both stressed and overwhelmed, it's about your narrative of emotional and mental depletion - there's just too much going on to manage effectively.

Anxiety is an emotion characterized by feelings of tension, worried thoughts and physical changes like increased blood pressure. It is both a state and a trait.

Intolerance for uncertainty is an important contributing factor to all types of anxiety.

Worry is the thinking part of anxiety. It's a chain of negative thoughts about bad things that might happen in the future.

Vulnerability is the emotion we experience during times of uncertainty, risk, and emotional exposure.

There is no courage without vulnerability. Courage requires the willingness to lean into uncertainty, risk and emotional exposure.

Answer the following questions

1. Your daughter comes home from school and she says she's tired. You ask if she's stressed or overwhelmed and she asks you if there's any difference. Explain it to her with examples.

_____
_____
_____
_____
_____
_____
_____
_____

2. Stressful situations cause psychological and physiological reactions.

True [ ]   False [ ]

3. Stress leads to rise in heart rate and cortisol.

True [ ]   False [ ]

4. You made a new friend in the neighborhood. He runs three to four jobs daily and you can see he is constantly stressed. You tell him to watch it and he says there's nothing to watch about it. Tell him the downsides of continuous stress.

_____
_____
_____
_____
_____
_____
_____
_____

5. What's the best way to manage getting overwhelmed? Is it giving up, taking a break, travelling? Mention what to do when you feel overwhelmed

_____
_____
_____
_____
_____
_____
_____
_____
_____

6. You take a visit to see your aunt who is a workaholic. You find out she recently lost her fiancée and she comes back from work on that day overwhelmed yet she has a lot of work waiting for her. Tell her to engage in non-doing and explain its benefit to her.

_____
_____
_____
_____
_____
_____
_____
_____

7. When your emotions are intense, your focus is moderate and your clarity about what you're feeling is low, you're _____

a. confused

b. stressed

c. tired

d. overwhelmed

8. Very high loss of control, thoughts about the worst-case scenario in every situation and complete uncertainty describe _____

a. overwhelmed

b. anxiety

c. anger

d. mood swing

9. Tick the right boxes

Which of the following are signs of anxiety?

Worry	[ ]
Overeating	[ ]
Bloating	[ ]
Irritability	[ ]
Constant desire to be in control	[ ]
Muscle tension	[ ]
Insomnia	[ ]
Obesity	[ ]
Anger	[ ]
Avoidance	[ ]

10. What's the best way to deal with worry and avoidance? Is it by taking a nap or doing other interesting things? Mention them.

_____
_____
_____
_____
_____

_____
_____

11. Why is it important to label your feelings?

_____
_____
_____
_____
_____
_____
_____
_____

12. Vulnerability is not weakness. It's our greatest measure of courage.

True [ ]   False [ ]

#2 PLACES WE GO WHEN WE COMPARE

Here are a few key takeaways from this section

Comparison drives all sorts of big feelings that can affect our relationship and self-worth.

Comparison is the crush of conformity from one side and competition from the other – it's trying to simultaneously stand out and fit in.

Even if we do not choose whether or not to make a comparison, we can choose whether or not to let that comparison affect our mood or self perceptions.

We feel admiration when someone's abilities, accomplishments or character inspires us or when we see something else that inspires us, like art or nature. Reverence is a deeper form of admiration or respect and is often combined with a sense of meaningful connection with something greater than ourselves.

Envy is when we want something that someone else has while jealousy is when we fear losing something valuable.

Schadenfreude is pleasure derived from someone else's misfortune. It's an emotion born out of inferiority not superiority.

Answer the following questions

1. Significant parts of our lives including our future are shaped by comparing ourselves to others.

True [ ]   False [ ]

2. While volunteering to help teenagers, you meet a girl who's a social media influencer. She became popular and rich by criticizing others and comparing herself to others. She doesn't know why she's angry, fearful and sad. Explain to her how social comparisons

Can envy + jealousy be switched through mindset to inspiration/admiration?

work and why she needs to choose connection instead of comparison.

_____
_____
_____
_____
_____
_____
_____
_____

3. Our hardwiring makes us default to comparison – it seems to happen to us rather than be our choice.

True [ ]   False [ ]

4. Admiration fosters self-betterment; reverence seems to foster a desire for connection to what we revere.

True [ ]   False [ ]

5. Your son comes home sulking. He says his friend has a better toy then him. You want to know if its jealousy or envy but he doesn't know the difference. Explain it to him and the effects.

_____
_____
_____
_____
_____
_____
_____

6. Tick the right boxes

Which of the following leads to envy?

Attraction   [ ]

Who inspired me?

Social skills [ ]

Competence [ ]

Position or ranking [ ]

Wealth [ ]

Intellect [ ]

Hostility [ ]

7. You have a set of twins, an 8 year old boy and girl. Some of their friends come around for a sleep over and you speak to them about acknowledging their feelings. Tell them the benefits.

_____
_____
_____
_____
_____
_____
_____
_____

8. Fill in the gap truthfully

It's really important for me not to be perceived as _____

9. What's the reason for your answer in the previous question? How can you improve or get over the feeling?

_____
_____
_____
_____
_____
_____

10. Your cousin and his friends are working against another team for their science project. Some of your cousin's friends have spotted mistakes in the other team and they take pleasure in it. Explain to them the dangers of schadenfreude.

_____
_____
_____
_____
_____
_____
_____

11. Freudenfreude is a subset of empathy

True [ ]   False [ ]

12. How do you strengthen freudenfreude instead of schadenfreude? Write out your plan for one week.

_____
_____
_____
_____
_____
_____
_____
_____

#3 PLACES WE GO WHEN THINGS DON'T GO AS PLANNED

Here are a few key takeaways from this section

Boredom is the uncomfortable state of wanting to engage in satisfying activity but being unable to do it.

Not all experiences of boredom are negative. Boredom is your imagination calling out to you.

Disappointment is unmet expectations. When we develop expectations, we paint a picture in our head of how things are going to be and how they're going to look.

When someone shares their dream with us, we are witnessing deep courage and vulnerability.

Feeling discouraged and resigned is about effort than outcome. Discouragement encourages us to lose motivation and confidence to continue with our efforts while resignation makes us lose the motivation to keep trying.

Disappointments may be like paper cuts, but if the cuts are deep enough or if we accumulate them over a lifetime, they can leave us seriously wounded.

It takes courage to reality-check, communicate, and dig into the intentions behind our expectations, but an exercise in vulnerability helps us maintain meaningful connection with ourselves and others.

Answer the following questions

1. When we're bored we experience a lack of simulation, time seems to pass very slowly.

True [ ]   False [ ]

2. Tick the right boxes

Which of the following are signs of boredom?

Laziness [ ]

Excitement [ ]

Frustration [ ]

Anger [ ]

Restlessness [ ]

Sleepy [ ]

Hungry [ ]

Lethargy [ ]

3. Can you recall a recent task you were meant to manage but you were bored while at it? What was the task, how long did it take you to finish the task and how did you get out of the boredom? Did it help you become more imaginative?

_____
_____
_____
_____
_____
_____
_____
_____

4. The more significant the expectation, the more significant the disappointment

True [ ]   False [ ]

5. Your son comes home from school and he tells you he's disappointed in himself because his science project didn't work out well. He feels ashamed and he says he doesn't want to go back to school again. How can you help him get over his disappointment?

Will you help him see that some expectations are beyond his control, or cook him his favorite meal or spend some time with him? What will you do?

_____
_____
_____
_____
_____
_____
_____
_____

6. Your eighteen year old niece is in a relationship and she has great expectations but you can see they are unrealistic and they would lead to disappointment, heartbreak and anger. What questions can you ask her to help her see she's only preparing for disappointment and hurt?

_____
_____
_____
_____
_____
_____
_____
_____

7. Why is it important to reality-check your expectations?

_____
_____
_____
_____
_____
_____
_____

8. Do you think moments of disappointment are moments to bond or connect with others?

Yes [ ]   No [ ]

9. Explain the reason for your answer

_____
_____
_____
_____
_____
_____
_____
_____

10. You made a new friend with a ten year old girl who has experienced so much disappointment from people in her life that she has decided to live in disappointment than take any risk. How can you help her? Will you help her see the difference between disappointment, regret, discouragement, resignation and frustration? What will you do?

_____
_____
_____
_____
_____
_____
_____
_____

11. You become a volunteer at a nursing home. You met a senior who told you about her disappointment and regret. You notice she uses the words interchangeably. Explain the difference between the two words.

_____
_____
_____
_____
_____
_____
_____
_____
_____

12. Have you ever had regrets? If your answer is yes, reflect and write out the good things or things you learned from it.

_____
_____
_____
_____
_____
_____
_____
_____

#4 PLACES WE GO WHEN IT'S BEYOND US

Here are a few key takeaways from this section

Both awe and wonder are often experienced in response to nature, art, music, spiritual experiences or ideas. Wonder inspires the wish to understand; awe inspires the wish to let shine, to acknowledge and to unite.

Confusion is critical to knowledge acquisition and learning.

Curiosity is an irreducible component of courageous leadership. It is recognizing a gap in our knowledge about something that interests us and becoming emotionally and cognitively invested in closing that gap through learning. It begins with interest and can range from mild curiosity to passionate investigation.

Surprise is an interruption caused by information that doesn't fit with our current understanding and expectations.

Answer the following questions

1. Your son's school took your twin boys, John, James and their classmates to NASA and they saw many things that inspired them. You could see how happy they were when they got home. John says he wants to be an astronaut and James writes a poem from his experience to encourage more people to become astronauts. Who is in wonder and who is in awe? Explain the reason for your answer.

_____
_____
_____
_____
_____
_____

2. Wonder fuels our passion for curiosity, learning and adventure

True [ ]   False [ ]

3. Can you share personal but simple experiences that have left you in awe?

4. How can confusion be a good thing?

5. Your visit your cousin. Her daughter is working on a music assignment from school. You notice she's confused. How can you help her to prevent confusion moving into frustration and giving up?

_____
_____
_____

7. Tick the right boxes

Which of the following can be used to resolve confusion?

Finding a hobby [ ]

Learning anew [ ]

Seeking help [ ]

Taking a break [ ]

Finding the most important thing [ ]

Playing a game [ ]

A movie break [ ]

Monitoring progress [ ]

Planning a strategy [ ]

Taking a walk [ ]

8. Curiosity and interest are both important parts of our need for meaning-making

True [ ]   False [ ]

9. Curiosity involves emotion and cognition (feeling and thinking) while interest covers only thinking or cognition.

True [ ]   False [ ]

10. What's the connection between curiosity and vulnerability?

_____
_____
_____

_____
_____
_____
_____
_____

11. Your friend is taking up a leadership position in school. He asks you what traits he needs the most to thrive as a leader. Mention one and the reason why you chose it.

_____
_____
_____
_____
_____
_____
_____
_____

#5 PLACES WE GO WHEN THINGS AREN'T WHAT THEY SEEM

Here are a few key takeaways from this section

As humans, it is completely normal to feel competing emotions and contradictory thoughts which can be messy, uncomfortable, vulnerable and irritating.

There's nothing more limiting than tapping out of tension and oversimplifying the thoughts and feelings that have the power to help us understand who we are and what we need.

Acknowledging uncertainty is a function of grounded confidence.

Amusement is connected to humor and includes elements of unexpectedness, incongruity, and playfulness. It is pleasurable, relaxed excitation.

Bittersweet is a mixed feeling of happiness and sadness.

Nostalgia is a double-edge sword, a tool for both connection and disconnection. It is a yearning for the way things used to be in our often idealized and self-protective version of the past.

Rumination is an involuntary focus on negative and pessimistic thoughts; reflection is highly adaptive and psychologically healthy. Rumination is a strong predicator of depression, making us more likely to pay attention to negative things, and zaps our motivation to do things that would improve how we feel.

Cognitive dissonance is a state of tension that occurs when a person holds two cognitions (ideas, attitudes, beliefs, opinions) that are psychologically inconsistent with each other. Dissonance produces mental discomfort that ranges from minor pangs to deep anguish; people don't rest easy till they find a way to reduce it.

Paradox challenges us to straddle the tension of two conflicting elements and recognize that they can both be true.

Answer the following questions

1. Complexity is one of our greatest teachers.

True [ ]   False [ ]

2. Your cousin comes home from college and tells you she wants to drop out because things are getting too complex for her to handle. Help her see the beauty of complexity and how to handle complexity.

_____
_____
_____
_____
_____
_____
_____
_____

3. When we gather information from our emotions, thoughts, and behaviors, especially the layered, messy ones, the tension can serve us.

True [ ]   False [ ]

4. Your teenage son is head over heels in love. He tells you about it but he subtly mentions his uncertainties. You can see he's trying to cover up his uncertainties. Explain the importance of sharing uncertainties.

_____
_____
_____
_____
_____
_____
_____

5. What's the difference between amusement and happiness?

6. There's a new employee in the firm you're working. He's a quiet person. Today at lunch break, you sit by him and find him very amusing. You ask why he's quiet and he says everyone is always busy and keeping to themselves. Tell him why amusement is beneficial irrespective of what others do.

7. Can you describe the recent bittersweet experience you had?

_____
_____

8. Tick the right boxes

Which of the following can trigger nostalgia?

Quest for meaning　　　　　　[ ]

Breaking up from a relationship　　[ ]

Losing loved ones　　　　　　[ ]

Finding new hobbies　　　　　[ ]

Negative moods　　　　　　　[ ]

Loneliness　　　　　　　　　[ ]

9. You are a volunteer at a children and teenagers camp and you're helping them understand emotions. Someone asks you the difference between rumination, reflection and worry. Help them understand it.

_____
_____
_____
_____
_____
_____
_____
_____

10. The greater the magnitude of the dissonance, the greater is the pressure to reduce dissonance.

True [ ]   False [ ]

11. Your grandfather doesn't believe two contrary opinions can be true at once. Use an example to explain how paradoxes exist.

_____
_____
_____
_____
_____
_____
_____
_____
_____

12. Your two kids are playful and they can be sarcastic when speaking with you. Explain to them the need to watch sarcasm and irony as well as the right context for both.

_____
_____
_____
_____
_____
_____
_____
_____
_____

#6 PLACES WE GO WHEN WE ARE HURTING

Here are a few key takeaways from this section

Anguish is an almost unbearable and traumatic swirl of shock, incredulity, grief, and powerlessness. It causes us to physically crumple in ourselves bringing us to our knees or forcing us all the way to the ground.

Hope is a warm, fuzzy emotion that fills us with a sense of possibility. It's a function of struggle; we develop hope not during the easy or comfortable times, but through adversity and discomfort.

Hope is learned.

Hopelessness arises out of a combination of negative life events and negative thought patterns, particularly self blame and the perceived inability to change our circumstances.

Hopelessness can apply to a specific situation or to life. Despair is a sense of hopelessness about a person's entire life and future.

To be human is to know sadness. Owning our sadness is courageous and a necessary step in finding ourselves and each other.

Grief is a process that includes many emotions rather than a single emotion. Grief doesn't necessarily progress in predictable sequenced stages. A central process in grieving is the attempt to reaffirm or reconstruct a world of meaning that has been challenged by loss.

Answer the following questions

1. Anguish not only takes away our ability to breathe, feel, and think. It comes for our bones.

True [ ]   False [ ]

2. The element of powerlessness is what makes anguish traumatic

True [ ]   False [ ]

3. Your old school friend moves into your neighborhood. You were bff's and you begin to pick it up again. She just had her baby but it was a stillborn. A few weeks later her husband moved on with some other woman. Do you think she's in pain or anguish? Explain the reason for your answer.

_____
_____
_____
_____
_____
_____
_____
_____

4. Why do people prefer not to process the trauma of anguish? Is it because they are fine, they are strong or they live in denial? Mention the reasons

_____
_____
_____
_____
_____
_____
_____
_____

5. Tick the right boxes

Which of the following makes us experience hope?

Having faith in yourself   [ ]

Setting goals [ ]

Setting realistic goals [ ]

Planning [ ]

Executing goals [ ]

Sticking to the plan with no alternative [ ]

Creating flexible plans [ ]

Relaxing when you need to [ ]

Finding your passion [ ]

Believing in yourself [ ]

6. You make a new teenage friend at the park. He believes hope is overrated. Explain why it isn't.

_____
_____
_____
_____
_____
_____
_____
_____

7. How can your children learn to build hope? What is your role in helping our children learn hope? What can you do?

_____
_____
_____
_____
_____
_____

_____
_____

8. Tick the right boxes

Hopelessness is caused by

Disappointment　　　　　　　　[ ]

Unrealistic goals　　　　[ ]

Inordinate ambition　　　[ ]

Inability to execute goals　[ ]

Disappointment　　　　　　　　[ ]

Constant failure　　　　　　　[ ]

Not believing in yourself　[ ]

9. Can you remember specific situations when you felt despair and when you felt hopelessness? Differentiate between the two.

_____
_____
_____
_____
_____
_____
_____

10. You're speaking with a group of fourth graders about resilience. Tell them how to build resilience.

_____
_____
_____
_____
_____

_____
_____
_____

11. Has there ever been a time where you've been sad but it helped you? Can you describe such experience and what you learned?

_____
_____
_____
_____
_____
_____
_____
_____

12. Have you ever been through grief? Can you identify the process of loss, longing and feeling lost? Write it out.

_____
_____
_____
_____
_____
_____
_____
_____

—

#7 PLACES WE GO WITH OTHERS

Here are a few key takeaways from this section

Compassion is fueled by understanding and accepting that we are all made of strength and struggle, no one is immune to pain or suffering. It is a practice based in the beauty and pain of shared humanity.

Compassion is a daily practice and empathy is a skill set that is one of the most powerful tools of compassion.

Instead of feeling the openness of compassion, pity makes you see others as different yourself. It sets up a separation between yourself and others, a sense of distance and remoteness from the suffering of others that is affirming and gratifying to the self.

Pity involves four elements: a belief that the suffering person is inferior; a passive self-focused reaction that does not include providing help; a desire to maintain emotional distance; and avoidance of sharing in the person's suffering.

Sympathy makes someone stand at a safe distance of 'not me' to relate with you instead of conveying the 'me too' that comes with empathy. Sympathy can be a trigger for shame.

The heart of compassion is acceptance

Boundaries are a prerequisite for compassion and empathy.

Answer the following questions

1. Compassion is a practice of 'better than' or I can fix you.

True [ ]   False [ ]

2. Compassion is the daily practice of recognizing and accepting our shared humanity so that we can treat ourselves and others with loving kindness and we take action in the face of suffering.

True [ ]   False [ ]

3. Your son wants to be a volunteer worker for people who lost their homes in a flood. He's read about compassion and empathy but he can't tell the difference. Explain it to him.

_____
_____
_____
_____
_____
_____
_____

4 Which of these moms is more compassionate? Maggie who always makes sure are kids are perfect, they never lack anything and she's always there for them to fix any problem or Jane who takes out the time to sit and listen to her kids' challenges without 'fixing it' even though they make mistakes and they lack a few things.

_____
_____
_____
_____
_____
_____
_____

5. Pity is a near enemy of compassion

True [ ]   False [ ]

6. Tick the right boxes

Compassion makes you experience a person's pain without touching it   [ ]

Pity brings a dividing wall between you and others.
[ ]

If pity was a person it will point and say you while compassion says us   [ ]

Compassion makes you become like others
[ ]

Pity can give you an exhilarating feeling because you're not the one who's being focused on   [ ]

Compassion doesn't guarantee connecting with others
[ ]

Everyone needs to pity and show pity
[ ]

Empathy is the spine of compassion
[ ]

7. Your younger cousin is such a sweet girl. When people who are close to her are in pain, she feels it and it sometimes leads her into despair and depression. Explain the dangers of this and tell her about compassion, cognitive empathy and compassion.

_____
_____
_____
_____
_____
_____
_____
_____

8. Would you say sympathy is the opposite of empathy or a near enemy of sympathy? Explain the reason for your answer

_____
_____

_____
_____
_____
_____
_____
_____

9. Your daughter comes back from school and asks you, how can I connect to someone's experience without walking in their shoes? What would you tell her? Would you tell her to focus on herself, learn to believe in others, or learn to listen attentively? What would you say?

_____
_____
_____
_____
_____
_____
_____

10. Your niece is staying with you for the holidays. Her old school friend visits her and she does the same. She's quick to help her friend because they used to be bff's but her friend doesn't see her as a bff anymore. Explain the importance of boundaries to her.

_____
_____
_____
_____
_____
_____
_____

11. The better we are at accepting ourselves and others, the more compassionate we become.

True [ ]   False [ ]

12. Your neighbor's son says he's tired of being run over and used by his friends. Join him to write out his boundaries for his friends

_____
_____
_____
_____
_____
_____
_____
_____
_____
_____

#8 PLACES WE GO WHEN WE FALL SHORT

Here are a few key takeaways from this section

Shame says I'm bad. The focus is on self. The result is feeling flawed and unworthy of love, belonging and connection.

Guilt says I did something bad and the focus is on the behavior. Guilt is the discomfort we feel when we evaluate what we've done or failed to do against our values. Remorse is a subset of guilt, it is what we feel when we harmed someone else or when we feel bad about an action and atone for a behavior.

Humiliation is what you feel when you've been belittled or put down by someone. This leaves you feeling unworthy of connection and disgusted with myself.

Embarrassment is fleeting and sometimes funny. It makes you feel uncomfortable but you know that you're not alone because everyone does these kinds of things.

Self-compassion is the first step to healing shame. We need to be kind to ourselves before we can share our stories with someone else. Self-compassion involves self-kindness, common humanity and mindfulness.

Healthy striving is internally driven while perfectionism is externally driven by a simple but potentially all-consuming question which is 'What would people think?' Perfectionalism tells us that our mistakes and failures are personal failures so we either avoid trying new things or we barely recover every time we inevitably fall short.

Answer the following questions

1. Shame drives positive change

True [ ]   False [ ]

2. Humiliation makes you feel that you deserve a sense of unworthiness

True [ ]   False [ ]

3. Your son comes home from school sulking. He made a mistake in his math test so he didn't pass it. He believes he is the dumbest person on earth and he doesn't think anyone feels what he does. He prefers to not talk about it and lock himself in his bedroom. Explain why he needs to speak up about it.

_____
_____
_____
_____
_____
_____
_____
_____

4. What can be used to replace shame since it's born out of fear of disconnection? What two emotions can be used to help your son gain a sense of connection?

_____

5. Tick the right boxes

Which of the following sentences is correct?

Shame thrives on secrecy, silence and judgment
  [ ]

Empathy is the best antidote to shame
  [ ]

Once you believe no one understands, shame takes over
  [ ]

Self-compassion is the only tool you need to get over shame
[ ]

Shame can heal on its own
[ ]

Shame happens between people and heals between them
[ ]

Shame is the lens through which I think others view me
[ ]

6. You can hear your younger sister and her friends talk about self-kindness, self-criticism and self-judgment. They've got it all mixed it and they are asking you to explain it. Do this for them and link it to self-compassion.

_____
_____
_____
_____
_____
_____
_____
_____
_____

7. Would you say self-kindness is easy, difficult or self-revolutionary? Explain the reason for your answer.

_____
_____
_____
_____
_____
_____
_____
_____

8. Get a pen and notepad. Think back to your earliest memories of shame and to the recent ones. Look for something that is similar in all the events. There's something that triggers shame. What is it? Look through the experiences and write them down. How realistic are these thoughts and can you identify someone to share these thoughts with?

_____
_____
_____
_____
_____
_____
_____
_____
_____

9. Perfectionism and shame go hand in hand.

True [ ]   False [ ]

10. You're helping your kids identify and understand their emotions. Help them see the difference between shame and guilt with one of their daily experience and how shame makes you doubt yourself so you don't believe you can change.

_____
_____
_____
_____
_____
_____
_____
_____
_____

#9

PLACES WE GO WHEN WE SEARCH FOR CONNECTION

Here are a few key takeaways from this section

We have to belong to ourselves as much as we need to belong to others. Any belonging that asks us to betray ourselves is not true belonging. True belonging doesn't require us to change who we are; it requires us to be who we are.

Belonging uncertainty is a more general inference, drawn from cues, events, experiences, and relationships, about the quality of fit or potential fit between oneself and a setting.

Connection is the energy that exists between people when they feel seen, heard, and valued; when they can give and receive without judgment; and when they derive sustenance and strength from the relationship.

Self-security is the open and non-judgmental acceptance of one's own weaknesses.

Invisibility is a function of disconnection and dehumanization, where an individual or group's humanity and relevance are unacknowledged, ignored, and/or diminished in value or importance.

Loneliness is perceived social isolation. At the heart of loneliness is the absence of meaningful social interaction – an intimate relationship, friendships, family gatherings, or even community or work group connections. It's not the quantity of friends that matters but the quality of a few relationships that actually matters.

Answer the following questions

1. Finding a sense of belonging in close relationships and with our community is essential to well-being.

True [ ]   False [ ]

2. Your niece wants to join the cheerleaders in her school. They tell her to abandon her style and the things she likes in order to be considered a part of them. Explain to her what true belonging is.

_____
_____
_____
_____
_____
_____
_____

3. You're speaking to a couple of teenagers about the need to be true to themselves. Explain to them how vulnerability, self-acceptance and our sense of belonging work hand in hand.

_____
_____
_____
_____
_____
_____
_____

4. Can you talk about an experience of disconnection that you had that was so painful?

_____
_____
_____
_____
_____
_____
_____

5. From your experience in the previous number use your words to define disconnection.

_____
_____
_____
_____
_____
_____
_____
_____

6. What's the best thing to do when you experience disconnection? How can you strengthen connection?

_____
_____
_____
_____
_____
_____
_____
_____

7. Tick the right boxes

Which of the following statements are true?

Feeling disconnected continually can lead to depression and suicide   [ ]

Disconnection leads to social isolation   [ ]

Social isolation leads to disconnection   [ ]

Recognizing and talking about disconnection helps   [ ]

Pain and hurt from disconnection can have deeper effect
[ ]

Pain and hurt from disconnection are more than physical pain
[ ]

8. Your neighbor's son had to leave the school's soccer team because of the feelings of disconnection and bullying even though he loves soccer. He keeps telling everyone it's no big deal and he acts it by pretending he doesn't need anyone. Tell him the dangers of what he's doing.

_____
_____
_____
_____
_____
_____
_____
_____
_____

9. How can perfectionism lead to disconnection?

_____
_____
_____
_____
_____
_____
_____
_____

10. In what ways have you experienced invisibility? Share an experience that affected someone close to you.

_____
_____
_____

_____
_____
_____
_____
_____

11. Do you think it is possible to be in the midst of family and friends yet feel lonely?

Yes [ ]   No [ ]

12. Give reasons for your answer in the previous question

_____
_____
_____
_____
_____
_____
_____
_____
_____

#10 PLACES WE GO WHEN THE HEART IS OPEN

Here are a few key takeaways from this section

Love is an emotion that we're capable of feeling in many different contexts from intimate partner relationships and family bonds to friends and pets.

Heartbreak is what happens when love is lost. Every time we love we risk heartbreak.

The heartbroken are the bravest among us, they dared to love.

Trust is choosing to risk making something you value vulnerable to another person's actions. Distrust means you believe what is important to you isn't safe with another.

Self-trust is normally the first casualty of failure or mistakes. We stop trusting ourselves when we hurt others, get hurt, feel shame, or question our worth.

Betrayal is so painful because at its core is a violation of trust.

Defensiveness is a way to protect our ego and a fragile self-esteem. Self-esteem is considered fragile when our failures, mistakes and imperfections decrease our self-worth.

Defensiveness blocks us from hearing feedback and evaluating if we want to make meaningful changes in our thinking or behavior based on input from others.

Flooding is when you feel physically and mentally overwhelmed during conflict and it hinders a productive and fruitful discussion.

When people feel hurt, they have appraised something that someone said or di as causing them emotional pain.

Answer the following questions

1. Tick the right boxes

Love is something your receive only [ ]

Love is something you can only receive when you give it [ ]

Love is something that we must nurture and grow [ ]

Love is a deep connection between those you care for [ ]

Love comes with trust, respect, kindness and affection [ ]

Love only exists between people who are intimate [ ]

Love must be carefully cultivated [ ]

You can stumble into love [ ]

2. Your son comes home from school and asks you what real love is? Explain it to him.

_____
_____
_____
_____
_____
_____
_____
_____

3. Shame, blame, disrespect, betrayal and the withholding of affection damage the roots from which love grows.

True [ ]   False [ ]

4. Can you share the most profound experience of love you've ever had that if someone had told you about it before it happened you would definitely doubt it?

_____
_____
_____
_____
_____
_____
_____
_____
_____

5. Go through the news for today. Identify one news story that an ethics of love would have changed that story or prevented it from happening.

_____
_____
_____
_____
_____
_____
_____
_____

6. Heartbreak is synonymous with disappointment because you feel the same kind of pain.

True [ ]   False [ ]

7. Tick the right boxes

Rejection leads to heartbreak

Lack of boundaries leads to heartbreak
        [ ]

You're heartbroken when the love you give isn't reciprocated
        [ ]

Unrequited love can't lead to heartbreak   [ ]

Death leads to heartbreak   [ ]

Disappointment is a major cause of heartbreak
[ ]

Consistent heartbreak can lead to lack of vulnerability
[ ]

Loss of love can lead to permanent heartbreak
[ ]

8. You're speaking to teenagers at a camp about trust. One of them asks you what exactly makes us trust. What would you tell them? The elements of trust, love, loveliness, or disappointments? Mention them.

_____
_____
_____
_____
_____
_____
_____
_____
_____

9. What's the worst form of betrayal you've experience? Is it betrayal from friends or family or yourself?

_____
_____

10. Why do people try to cover-up after betrayal?

_____
_____
_____
_____
_____
_____
_____
_____

11. Defensiveness occurs in aspects of our lives where our self-esteem is really fragile

True [ ]   False [ ]

12. Your son was fighting in school. It turns out he was defensive over something he did wrong. You let him know and he acknowledges it. He asks you how to prevent it from happening again. What would you tell him? Would you help him identify physical cues from the last time he was defensive or tell him to walk away or open his palms or take a deep breath?

_____
_____
_____
_____
_____
_____
_____
_____
_____

#11 PLACES WE GO WHEN LIFE IS GOOD

Here are a few key takeaways from this section

Joy is sudden, unexpected, short-lasting, and high-intensity. It's characterized by a connection with others, or with God, nature, or the universe. Joy expands our thinking and attention, and it fills us with a sense of freedom and abandon.

Happiness is stable, longer-lasting, and normally the result of effort. It's lower in intensity than joy and more self-focused. With happiness, we feel a sense of being in control. Unlike joy, which is more internal, happiness seems more external and circumstantial.

The relationship between joy and gratitude is an intriguing upward spiral.

Calm creates a perspective and mindfulness while managing emotional reactivity.

Contentment is about satisfaction. It's the feeling of completeness, appreciation and enoughness that we experience when our needs are satisfied.

Gratitude is an emotion that reflects our deep appreciation for what we value, what brings meaning to our lives, and what makes us feel connected to ourselves and others. Gratitude helps us to extract benefits from our experiences and we're less likely to take it for granted.

If you're afraid to lean into good news, wonderful moments and joy, its forebrooding joy and most people experience it.

Relief is when feelings of tension leave the body and being able to breathe more easily, thoughts of the worst being over and being safe for the moment, resting and wanting to get on to something else.

Tranquility is associated with the absence of demand and no pressure to do anything.

Contentment comes with having completing something. Tranquility helps you relish the feeling of doing nothing.

Answer the following questions

1. When we experience joy we lose ourselves

True [ ]   False [ ]

2. Take your mind back to the last time you felt joy. What was your body posture and how did you feel?

_____
_____
_____
_____
_____
_____
_____
_____

3. Using your experiences, can you differentiate between happiness and joy?

_____
_____
_____
_____
_____
_____
_____
_____

4. Calm has the ability to heal and quieten us from within

True [ ]   False [ ]

5. Are there things everyone has always believed to be a reason for contentment but you didn't get content when you did it?

Yes [ ]   No [ ]

6. What was it and why weren't you content? Was it as a result of disappointment, unmet expectations, bittersweet experiences or what you experienced didn't satisfy a part of you? Mention your reasons.

_____
_____
_____
_____
_____
_____
_____
_____

7. What brings contentment and fulfillment?

_____
_____
_____
_____
_____
_____
_____
_____

8. It's bedtime for your kids. You always spend a few minutes giving them a few life nuggets before they sleep. Today, talk to them about gratitude and its benefits.

_____
_____
_____
_____
_____

9. Gratitude helps us hold on to the value of something so we can extract more benefits from it

True [ ]   False [ ]

10. What can you do to make gratitude a permanent practice and not just an emotion?

_____
_____
_____
_____
_____
_____
_____
_____

11. You take a sigh of relief and your son asks you why you do that and what you gain from it. Explain the benefits of relief to him.

_____
_____
_____
_____
_____
_____
_____
_____

12. Think of an environment that can help you create tranquility and create it. Work on it for one week and then one month and many more months.

_____
_____

#12 PLACES WE GO WHEN WE FEEL WRONGED

Here are a few key takeaways for this section

Anger is an emotion we feel when something gets in the way of a desired outcome or when we believe there's a violation of the way things should be.

Anger is a catalyst. Holding on to it will make us exhausted and sick, internalizing it will take away our joy and spirit, externalizing it will make us less effective in our attempts to create change and forge connection.

We all have the right and need to feel and own our anger.

Contempt is one of the most damaging of the four negative communication patterns that predict divorce. Contempt aims to insult and psychologically abuse your partner. With your words and body language, you're lobbing insults right into the heart of your partner's sense of self.

Contempt simply says I'm better than you and you're lesser than me.

With contempt we look down on a person and we want to exclude or ignore them. With disgust inferiority is the issue, the feeling is more physical, we want to avoid being poisoned (either literally or figuratively)

Disgust arises as a feeling of aversion towards something offensive. Disgust is worse than contempt because once a person is viewed with disgust, the judgment is permanent. With anger, an apology or an attempt to correct the situation can right the wrong but this can't happen with disgust.

Dehumanization is the psychological process of demonizing the enemy, making them seem less than human and hence not worthy of humane treatment.

Hate is a combination of various negative emotions including repulsion, disgust, anger, fear, and contempt.

Self-righteousness is the conviction that one's beliefs and behaviors are the most correct.

Answer the following questions

1. Regulating and coping with anger rather than holding on to or expressing chronic anger is crucial for the health of our brain and other organs in the body.

True [ ]   False [ ]

2. Anger is a secondary or indicator emotion that often conceals emotions that are harder to recognize, name or own.

True [ ]   False [ ]

3. How do you react when you get angry? What other emotions do you feel when you get angry? Is it pain, hurt, sadness or disappointment? Mention them.

_____
_____
_____
_____
_____
_____
_____
_____

4. Have you ever used anger to mask another emotion you felt? Why?

_____
_____
_____
_____
_____

5. Anger is a powerful catalyst but a life-sucking companion.

True [ ]   False [ ]

6. What signs show contempt from someone else to you or from you to someone else? Is it frowning, gossip, excommunication or hating? Mention all the signs.

_____
_____
_____
_____
_____
_____
_____

7. Tick the right boxes

Which of the following can evoke feelings of disgust?

Another person   [ ]

What we can feel with our senses [ ]

Unappealing food   [ ]

Another person's ideas   [ ]

Anger   [ ]

Bittersweet experience   [ ]

Shame   [ ]

Comedy   [ ]

Intense loathing [ ]

8. Your neighbor's son and your son are in the same class. They come home talking about slave trade and the treatment and dehumanization slaves endured. Your son attributes it to disgust while your neighbor's son says it is contempt. Explain to them what differentiates the two emotions.

_____
_____
_____
_____
_____
_____
_____
_____

9. To dehumanize someone means you have to make the person an enemy. What else is involved in the process of dehumanizing a person?

_____
_____
_____
_____
_____
_____
_____
_____

10. Your daughter has an essay to write and she needs your help. The essay is titled the beauty and ugly sides of language. Give her a few points with examples that she can build on.

_____
_____
_____
_____

11. Have you ever felt hate towards someone you don't know personally because they were part of a group or sect or something else? If you knew them personally or if they were in your class or they helped you at a point and you didn't know they were part of the sect, will your assessment of them remain the same? Why?

_____

12. Your granddaughter comes to you for help. She's trying to differentiate between self-righteousness and righteousness. Help her understand the difference.

#13 PLACES WE GO TO SELF-ASSESS

Here are a few key takeaways from this section

Pride is a feeling of pleasure or celebration related to our accomplishments or efforts. We take pride in what we've accomplished and this is called authentic pride. It is a feeling of pleasure or celebration related to our accomplishments or efforts.

Hubris is an inflated sense of one's own innate abilities that is tied more to the need for dominance than to actual accomplishments.

Narcissism is the shame-based fear of being ordinary.

Humility is openness to new learning combined with a balanced and accurate assessment of our contributions, including our strengths, imperfections, and opportunities for growth.

Intellectual humility is a willingness to consider information that doesn't fit with our current thinking.

Near enemies depict how spirituality can be misunderstood or misused to separate us from life.

True love allows, honors, and appreciates. Attachment grasps, demands, needs, and aims to possess.

It's the near enemies of connection – the imposters that can look and feel like cultivating closeness that sabotage relationships and leave us feeling alone and in pain.

Cultivating meaningful connection requires grounded confidence, the courage to walk alongside others, and story stewardship.

Embodiment is the awareness of our body's sensations, habits, and the beliefs that inform them. It requires the ability to feel and allow the body's emotions.

Disembodiment is an unawareness and repression of our sensations and emotions and/or privileging our thinking over our feeling. It leads to incongruence between the actions we take in the world and the beliefs that we hold.

Story stewardship means honoring the sacred nature of story, the ones we share and the ones we hear and knowing that we've been entrusted with something valuable or that we have something valuable that we should treat with respect and care.

Answer the following questions

1. The higher the hubris, the lower the self-esteem, and the higher the hubris, the higher the narcissism and shame-proneness.

True [ ]   False [ ]

2. You're watching TV with your nephew. He hears a presenter mention hubristic pride and authentic pride. He doesn't understand it. Explain the difference to him.

_____
_____
_____
_____
_____
_____
_____
_____

3. Tick the right boxes

People experiencing hubris feel superior
    [ ]

People observing hubristic people avoid them
        [ ]

From afar hubristic people look great and everyone wants to associate with them [ ]

Hubristic people are puffed up
[ ]

Hubristic people have an inferiority complex
[ ]

Hubristic people are arrogant and show dominance
[ ]

Shame and hubris go hand in hand
[ ]

Anxiety, aggression and hostility lead to hubris
[ ]

4. Your daughter comes back from college. She met Tracy her childhood friend over there. She says Tracy has changed as she has an air of superiority around her, she could feel a distance between herself and Tracy who didn't even try to smile at her. She doesn't know what it is. What do you think it is and can you explain it to your daughter?

_____
_____
_____
_____
_____
_____
_____
_____

5. You meet up your friends at the bar and Tim joins you guys. You find out he downplays all his achievements and doesn't act like he's rich or has accomplished so much even though he has. One of your friends says Tim is really humble. Is it humility? If it isn't what is it? Explain it.

_____
_____

_____
_____
_____
_____
_____
_____

6. Humility allows us to admit when we are wrong – we realize that getting it right is more important than needing to prove we are right.

True [ ]   False [ ]

7. Pride can be a good thing, hubris is dangerous and humility is key to grounded confidence and healthy relationships.

True [ ]   False [ ]

8. The near enemy of love is _____

a. affection

b. connection

c. attachment

9. The near enemy of equanimity is _____

a. jealousy

b. attachment

c. callousness

10. The near enemy of developing grounded confidence is _____

a. fragile self-worth

b. learning and improving

c. knowing and proving

11. What's the best way to distinguish if you're walking alongside or controlling the path

a. taking deep breaths

b. engaging your feelings

c. ask whose best interest you're protecting

12. What are the different types of power and what's the best for developing grounded confidence and connection?

_____
_____
_____
_____
_____
_____
_____
_____

13. The near enemy of practicing story stewardship is_____

a. Performing connection while driving disconnection

b. Non-performing connection

c. embodiment

14. Have you ever experienced narrative takeover? How did you feel about it?

_____
_____
_____
_____
_____
_____

_____
_____

15. The near enemy of narrative trust is_____

a. narrative sympathy

b. narrative distrust and diminishing the humanity of others

c. Narrative take over

Made in the USA
Monee, IL
26 September 2022